World's Greatest Riddles and Brain Teasers!

By

Edward Scarzi

Other books by Edward Scarzi:

World's Greatest Clean Jokes!

(Solutions are at the end of each section)

Discrete Reasoning Riddles

1. Isaac and Albert were excitedly describing the result of the Third Annual International Science Fair Extravaganza in Sweden. There were three contestants, Louis, Rene, and Johannes. Isaac reported that Louis won the fair, while Rene came in second. Albert, on the other hand, reported that Johannes won the fair, while Louis came in second. In fact, neither Isaac nor Albert had given a correct report of the results of the science fair. Each of them had given one correct statement and one false statement. What was the actual placing of the three contestants?

2. At a family reunion were the following people: one grandfather, one grandmother, two fathers, two mothers, four children, three grandchildren, one brother, two sisters, two sons, two daughters, one father-in-law, one mother-in-law, and one daughter-in-law. But not as many people attended as it sounds. How many were there, and who were they?

3. 97 baseball teams participate in an annual state tournament. The champion is chosen for this tournament by the usual elimination scheme. That is, the 97 teams are divided into pairs, and the two teams of each pair play against each other. The loser of each pair is eliminated, and the remaining teams

are paired up again, etc. How many games must be played to determine a champion?

4. Your sock drawer contains ten pairs of white socks and ten pairs of black socks. If you're only allowed to take one sock from the drawer at a time and you can't see what color sock you're taking until you've taken it, how many socks do you have to take before you're guaranteed to have at least one matching pair?

5. A man is the owner of a winery who recently passed away. In his will, he left 21 barrels (seven of which are filled with wine, seven of which are half full, and seven of which are empty) to his three sons. However, the wine and barrels must be split so that each son has the same number of full barrels, the same number of half-full barrels, and the same number of empty barrels. Note that there are no measuring devices handy. How can the barrels and wine be evenly divided?

6. What's the largest amount of money you can have in change and still not have change for a dollar?

7. What's the largest number of U.S. coins you can have without having even change for a dollar?

8. A man goes out for a walk. He walks south one mile, east one mile, and north one mile, and ends up in the same place he started. He didn't start out at the north pole -- so where did he?

9. A mountain goat attempts to scale a cliff sixty feet high. Every minute, the goat bounds upward three feet but slips back two. How long does it take for the goat to reach the top?

10. You have three boxes of fruit. One contains just apples, one contains just oranges, and one contains a mixture of both. Each box is labeled -- one says "apples," one says "oranges," and one says "apples and oranges." However, it is known that none of the boxes are labeled correctly. How can you label the boxes correctly if you are only allowed to take and look at just one piece of fruit from just one of the boxes?

11. An Arab sheikh is old and must will his fortune to one of his two sons. He makes a proposition. His two sons will ride their camels in a race, and whichever camel crosses the finish line last will win the fortune for its owner. During the race, the two brothers wander aimlessly for days, neither willing to cross the finish line. In desperation, they ask a wise man for advice. He tells them something; then the brothers leap onto the camels and charge toward the finish line. What did the wise man say?

12. You have a jug that holds five gallons, and a jug that holds three gallons. You have no other containers, and there are no markings on the jugs. You need to obtain exactly seven gallons of water from a faucet. How can you do it?
Second Problem: You need exactly four gallons. How do you do it?

13. You are on a game show. You are shown three closed doors. A prize is hidden behind one, and the game show host knows where it is. You are asked to select a door. You do. Before you open it, the host opens one of the other doors, showing that it is empty, then asks you if you'd like to change your guess. Should you, should you not, or doesn't it matter?

14. A farmer is taking a fox, a chicken, and a bag of grain home. To get there, he must cross a river, but he's only allowed to take one item across the bridge with them at a time. If the fox is left alone with the chicken, the fox will eat the chicken. If the chicken is left alone with the grain, the chicken will eat the grain. How can the farmer cross the river without any of his possessions being eaten?

15. Travelling to a city, an old man lost his way. He came to a fork in the road and did not know which road to take. Standing at the fork were two men. Next to the men was a sign, which you may assume is correct, which stated that one of the two men always told the truth and one of the men always told lies (but it was not known which was which). The sign went on to say that travelers could only ask one of the men one question.
What question could the old man pose that would give him the information he needs to choose the correct route?

16. You are given eight jelly doughnuts. The doughnuts all weigh the same amount except for one which is heavier. You have a balancing scale at your disposal. What's the minimum number of weighings required for you to pick out the heavy doughnut every time?

17. Three men stay at a hotel for the night. The innkeeper charges thirty dollars per room per night. The men rent one room; each pays ten dollars. The bellhop leads the men to their room. Later, the innkeeper discovers he has overcharged the men and asks the bellhop to return five dollars to them. On the way upstairs, the bellhop realizes that five dollars can't be evenly split among three men, so he decides to keep two dollars for himself and return one dollar to each man.
At this point, the men have paid nine dollars each, totaling 27. The bellhop has two, which adds up to 29. Where did the thirtieth dollar go?

18. Three men, members of a safari, are captured by cannibals in the jungle. The men are given one chance to escape with their lives. The men are lined up and bound to stakes such that one man can see the backs of the other two, the middle man can see the back of the front man, and the front man can't see anybody. The men are shown five hats, three of which are black and two of which are white. Then the men are blindfolded, and one of the five hats is placed on each man's head. The remaining two hats are hidden away. The blindfolds are removed. The men are told that if just one of the men can guess

what hat he's wearing, they may all go free. Time passes. Finally, the front man, who can't see anyone, correctly guesses the color of his hat. What color was it, and how did he guess correctly?

19. One day a girl celebrated her birthday. Two days later, her older twin brother celebrated his. How is this possible?

20. You and your spouse invite four other couples to a party. During the course of the conversation, it is discovered that, prior to the party, each person except you was acquainted with a different number of the people present. Assuming the acquaintance relationship is symmetric (i.e., if you are acquainted with someone, that person is also acquainted with you), then how many people did your spouse know prior to the party? How many people did you know?

21. A man is looking at a photograph of someone. His friend asks who it is. The man replies, "Brothers and sisters, I have none. But that man's father is my father's son." Who was in the photograph?

22. You have a 12 liter jug, an 8 liter jug, and a 5 liter jug. None of the jugs have any markings on them. The 12 liter jug is full, and the other two are empty. How can you divide the 12 liters of water equally (i.e., so two of the jugs have exactly 6 liters of water in them, and the third is empty)?

23. A gambler bet on a horse race, but the bookee wouldn't tell him the results of the race. The bookee

gave clues as to how the five horses finished --
which may have included some ties -- and wouldn't
pay the gambler off unless the gambler could
determine how the five horses finished based on the
following clues:
Penuche Fudge finished before Near Miss and after
Whispered Promises.
Whispered Promises tied with Penuche Fudge if and
only if Happy Go Lucky did not tie with Skipper's
Gal.
Penuche Fudge finished as many places after
Skipper's Gal as Skipper's Gal finished after
Whispered Promises if and only if Whispered
Promises finished before Near Miss.
The gambler thought for a moment, then answered
correctly. How did the five horses finish the race?

24. In a rectangular array of people, who will be
taller: the tallest of the shortest people in each
column, or the shortest of the tallest people in each
row?

25. You have two cups, one containing orange juice
and one containing and equal amount of lemonade.
One teaspoon of the orange juice is taken and mixed
with the lemonade. Then a teaspoon of this mixture
is mixed back into the orange juice. Is there more
lemonade in the orange juice or more orange juice
in the lemonade?

26. All of my flowers except two are roses. All of
my flowers except two are tulips. All of my flowers
except two are daisies. How many flowers do I have?

27. Three humans and three monkeys (one big, two small) need to cross a river. But there is only one boat, and it can only hold two bodies (regardless of their size), and only the humans or the big monkey are strong enough to row the boat. Furthermore, the number of monkeys can never outnumber the number of humans on the same side of the river, or the monkeys will attack the humans. How can all six get across the river without anyone getting hurt?

28. A computer cable has seven connectors, arranged in a perfect circle -- so by rotating the plug, it can be connected to the outlet in any of seven different ways. Each of the connectors is numbered from one to seven, each number being used exactly once. The same is true for the holes in the outlet. The device that uses this cable only requires that one of the connectors match up to its corresponding hole in order to operate. How should you number the connectors on the plug and the holes in the outlet so that, no matter how the cable is rotated and plugged in, at least one connector matches up?

29. Five men and five dogs (each man owned a dog) went hiking. They encountered a river that was swift and deep. The only way to cross it was an abandoned boat, left ashore on their side. But it would only hold three living things. Unfortunately, the dogs were edgy and could not be near another person (not even momentarily) unless its owner was present. One of the dogs attended a highly advanced, highly specialized obedience school and therefore

knew how to operate the boat -- the other dogs lack this skill. How did the five men and the five dogs cross the river?

30. On your travels, three men stand at a fork in the road. You're not sure which fork you need to take, but each of the three men do. One of these people tells the truth, one always lies, and the third tells the truth sometimes and lies the other times. Each of the three men know each of the others, but you don't know who is who. If you could ask only one of the men (chosen at random, since you don't know which man is which) one yes/no question, what question would you ask to determine the road you wish to take?

31. Abel, Mabel, and Caleb went bird watching. Each of them saw one bird that none of the others did. Each pair saw one bird that the third did not. And one bird was seen by all three. Of the birds Abel saw, two were yellow. Of the birds Mabel saw, three were yellow. Of the birds Caleb saw, four were yellow. How many yellow birds were seen in all? How many non-yellow birds were seen in all?

32. Four gentlemen (Adam, Bill, Chuck, and Dan) went to an expensive restaurant to dine. They checked their coats, hats, gloves, and canes at the door (each of the gentlemen had one of each). But when they checked out, there was a mix up, and each of the men ended up with exactly one article of clothing (a pair of gloves is considered a single article of clothing) belonging to each one of the four.

Adam and Bill ended up with their own coats, Chuck ended up with his own hat, and Dan ended up with his own gloves. Adam did not end up with Chuck's cane. State whose coat, hat, gloves, and cane each of the gentlemen ended up with.

33. A father is four times as old as his son. In twenty years, he'll be twice as old. How old are they now?

34. Four intellectuals are lined up so that each intellectual can see the ones in front of him but not the ones behind him. (The back one can see the other three, and the front one can't see anybody.) One hat is placed on the heads of each of the intellectuals. (None of them may see the color of their own hat, but each may see the color of the hats on the intellectuals in front of him.) Each of the four hats are one of three different colors (red, white, and blue), and there is at least one hat of each color (so there's one duplicate). Each of the intellectuals, starting with the back and ending with the front, is asked the color of the hat he is wearing. Each of the intellectuals is able to deduce and give a correct answer out loud, in turn. What arrangement of the hats permits this to be possible without guessing (since the specific colors chosen are arbitrary, just indicate which two intellectuals must be wearing hats of the same color), and how did they do it?

35. There are four men (call them 1, 2, 3, and 4) standing in front of a firing squad in a line. They are all facing the same direction such that 1 is at the

back of the line, and 4 is at the front. 1 and 3 are wearing black hats, and 2 and 4 are wearing white hats. Between 3 and 4 is a brick wall. So 1, at the back of the line, can see 2 and 3. 2 can see 3. Neither 3 and 4 can see anybody. The men know that two of them are wearing black hats and two of them are wearing white hats. The commander of the firing squad offers a challenge. The challenge is that he will let all of them go if only one of them correctly names the color of his own hat. The men are not allowed to talk amongst themselves. Which of the men know for sure the color of his hat?

36. How can you build pig pens so you can put nine pigs in four pens such that each pen has an odd number of pigs?

37. An explorer was trekking through a remote jungle when he was captured by logic-loving cannibals. He was brought before the chief and told, "You may now speak your last words. If your statement is true, then we will burn you at the stake. If your statement is false, we will boil you in oil." The man thought for a moment, then made his statement. Perplexed, the clever cannibals realized they could do nothing but let him go. What did the explorer tell them?

38. Three people go fishing -- two fathers and two sons. How is this possible?

39. Mr. Slow, Mr. Medium, Mr. Fast, and Mr. Speed must cross a rickety rope bridge in 17

minutes. The bridge can carry at most two people at a time. Furthermore, it's dark, and there is only one flashlight; any single person or pair of people crossing the bridge must have the flashlight with them. (The bridge is too wide for the flashlight to be thrown; it must be carried across.)

Each man walks at a different speed. A pair travelling together must walk at the rate of the slower man. Mr. Slow can cross the bridge in at most 10 minutes; Mr. Medium can cross in 5 minutes; Mr. Fast can cross in 2 minutes; Mr. Speed can cross in 1 minute. How do all four men get across in the bridge in 17 minutes?

40. You have twelve marbles. Eleven of the marbles are of equal weight, but one is heavier or lighter. You have a balancing scale you can use to find this marble and figure out if it weighs more or less than the others. What is the minimum number of weighings required to do this?

41. You have two slow-burning fuses, each of which will burn up in exactly one hour. They are not necessarily of the same length and width as each other, nor even necessarily of uniform width, so you can't measure a half hour by noting when one fuse is half burned. Using these two fuses, how can you measure 45 minutes?

42. You have an eight-gallon tank of water, which is completely full, an empty five-gallon tank, and an empty three-gallon tank. Without throwing any water away, can you put exactly four gallons in the

eight-gallon tank and four gallons in the five-gallon tank?

43. Five competitors -- A, B, C, D, and E -- enter a swimming race that awards gold, silver, and bronze medals to the first three to complete it. Each of the following compound statements about the race is *false*, although one of the two clauses in each *may* be true.
A didn't win the gold, and B didn't win the silver.
D didn't win the silver, and E didn't win the bronze.
C won a medal, and D didn't.
A won a medal, and C didn't.
D and E both won medals.
Who won each of the medals?

44. Two days ago, Suzy was 8. Next year, she'll be 11. How is this possible?

45. A man leaves home for a mountain at 1pm and reaches the top at 3pm. The following day he departs from the top at 1pm and gets home at 3pm, by following the same path as the day before. Was he necessarily ever at the same point on the path at the same time on both days?

Solutions for Discrete Reasoning Riddles

1. Johannes won; Rene came in second; Louis came in third.

2. There were two little girls and a boy, their parents, and their father's parents, totaling seven people.

3. 96. All teams but the champion team will lose a game exactly once.

4. Three. In the worst case, the first two socks you take out will consist of one black sock and one white sock. The next sock you take out is guaranteed to match one or the other.

5. Two half-full barrels are dumped into one of the empty barrels. Two more half-full barrels are dumped into another one of the empty barrels. This results in nine full barrels, three half-full barrels, and nine empty barrels. Each son gets three full barrels, one half-full barrel, and three empty barrels.

6. $1.19. Three quarters, four dimes, and four pennies.

7. Alternate Solution #1
Ninety nine -- if they're all pennies.
Alternate Solution #2
Actually, you can have any number. At one time, a U.S. $10 gold coin called the Eagle was minted, and

you could have any number of these without having change for a dollar. It is no longer minted, but it's still legal tender

8. Alternate Solution #1
Assuming a perfectly spherical Earth, somewhere one mile north of the latitude (in the southern hemisphere) that is one mile in circumference. The man walks south one mile to this latitude and walks one mile east, which takes him all the way around and back to where he started. The last step (one mile north) retraces the first step he took (one mile south).
Alternate Solution #2
The man could also be one mile north of the latitude that is one half mile in circumference -- on second leg of the journey, he'd go around twice instead of once. He could also be one mile north of the latitude that is one third of a mile in circumference, or one mile north of the latitude that is one quarter of a mile in circumference, and so on.

9. Fifty eight minutes. Although his net progress each minute is one foot, he reaches the top on the fifty-eighth minute just before he would normally slip back two feet.

10. Take a piece of fruit from the box marked "apples and oranges." Suppose the fruit you take is an apple. Then that box must be the box containing just apples. Therefore, the box marked "oranges" can't be the box containing just apples, and it can't be the box containing just oranges either -- so it

must be the box containing apples and oranges. The remaining box is therefore the box containing just oranges.

If the fruit you take out is an orange, the solution is derived in a similar fashion: the box marked "apples and oranges" is the box containing just oranges; the box marked "apples" is the box containing both apples and oranges; and the box marked "oranges" is the one containing just apples.

11. The rules of the race were that the owner of the *camel* that crosses the finish line last wins the fortune. The wise man simply told them to switch camels.

12. To get seven gallons, fill the five gallon jug and dump what you can into the three gallon jug, filling it. There are now two gallons in the five gallon jug. Dump out the three gallon jug, and put the two gallons from the five gallon jug into the three gallon jug. Then fill the five gallon jug. The total is seven gallons.

To get four gallons, fill the three gallon jug, and dump it into the five gallon jug. Fill the three gallon jug again, and dump what you can into the five gallon jug. Now there is one gallon in the three gallon jug. Dump out the five gallon jug, and put the one gallon from the three gallon jug into the five gallon jug. Now fill the three gallon jug. The total is four gallons.

13 Remember that the host *knows* where the prize is. When you pick a door, there's a 66.7% chance

you're wrong. If you're wrong, the host will *always* open the one door left that *doesn't* contain the prize. So if you were wrong (66.7% chance), you're better off switching to the door that the host leaves closed. What you are really being asked here is whether the odds are better with your first choice, or with *both* of the other two. All the host really does is prove that it isn't in one of the remaining two -- but we knew that anyway, because there's only one prize. Another way to look at it is this: consider that there are 1000 doors. You pick one. Before you open it, the host opens 998 of the 999 remaining doors. There's a 0.1% chance you guessed correctly -- if you guessed wrong (99.9% chance), then you *know* the prize is in the one door the host left shut. So you're better off changing your guess.

Still not convinced? This is *Brain Food*'s most contested answer, but it is correct! Let's break it down a little more explicitly:

There are nine possible scenarios:

Prize is behind door A. You pick door A.
Prize is behind door A. You pick door B.
Prize is behind door A. You pick door C.
Prize is behind door B. You pick door A.
Prize is behind door B. You pick door B.
Prize is behind door B. You pick door C.
Prize is behind door C. You pick door A.
Prize is behind door C. You pick door B.
Prize is behind door C. You pick door C.

Now the host, who knows which door the prize is behind, deliberately chooses a door that the prize is *not* behind. For the three cases where you chose correctly in the beginning, the host has the choice of which other door to open. It doesn't matter which one he picks. But for the six cases where you chose wrong, he deliberately chooses the wrong guess of the remaining two choices, revealing it to be a wrong guess. It all breaks down as follows:

Prize is behind door A. You pick door A. Host reveals door B or C as empty.

Prize is behind door A. You pick door B. Host reveals door C as empty.

Prize is behind door A. You pick door C. Host reveals door B as empty.

Prize is behind door B. You pick door A. Host reveals door C as empty.

Prize is behind door B. You pick door B. Host reveals door A or C as empty.

Prize is behind door B. You pick door C. Host reveals door A as empty.

Prize is behind door C. You pick door A. Host reveals door B as empty.

Prize is behind door C. You pick door B. Host reveals door A as empty.

Prize is behind door C. You pick door C. Host reveals door A or B as empty.

(We've had several complaints that the above listing is incorrect because scenarios 1, 5, and 9 should be broken out. In fact, it is incorrect to break them out, because what's important here is that each listed scenario have an equal probability of occurring, not that each scenario be broken down to irreducible terms.)

Now we come to the point where we must decide whether to stick to the original guess or to switch:

Prize is behind door A. You pick door A. Host reveals door B or C as empty. Switching loses.
Prize is behind door A. You pick door B. Host reveals door C as empty. Switching wins.
Prize is behind door A. You pick door C. Host reveals door B as empty. Switching wins.
Prize is behind door B. You pick door A. Host reveals door C as empty. Switching wins.
Prize is behind door B. You pick door B. Host reveals door A or C as empty. Switching loses.
Prize is behind door B. You pick door C. Host reveals door A as empty. Switching wins.
Prize is behind door C. You pick door A. Host reveals door B as empty. Switching wins.
Prize is behind door C. You pick door B. Host reveals door A as empty. Switching wins.
Prize is behind door C. You pick door C. Host reveals door A or B as empty. Switching loses.
Final conclusion: switching wins six out of nine times, which is equal to two thirds of the time, or about 66.7%.

14. Take the chicken across and leave it on the other side. Then go back. Get the fox and bring it to the other side and take the chicken back with you. Take the grain to the other side and leave it there. Then go back and get the chicken.

15. Alternate Solution #1
Ask one of the men what the other man would answer to the question, "Is the left road the correct road?" Then assume the answer you are given is false and act on that knowledge.

If the man you ask is the liar, he'll incorrectly give you the truthful man's answer. If the man you ask is the truthful man, he'll correctly give you the liar's wrong answer.

Alternate Solution #2

Ask one of the men, "If I had asked you which path was the correct path ten minutes ago, what would you have said?" Regardless of which man is asked this question, the answer will be the correct path.

16. Two. Weigh three of the doughnuts against three others and leave the remaining two on the table. If the scales are even, the heavy doughnut is one of the two on the table -- weigh them to find out. If the scales are uneven, take the three doughnuts on the heavy end, weigh one of them against another, and leave the third on the table. If the scales are uneven, you've found the heavy one. If not, the heavy one is the one on the table.

17. The mistake is in how the thirty dollars are accounted for. The two dollars that the bellhop has are part of the 27 the men have paid. A correct accounting of the money is that 27 dollars were paid and three dollars were not, totaling 30 dollars.

18. The back man can see the hats worn by the two men in front of him. So, if both of those hats were white, he would know that the hat he wore was black. But, since he doesn't answer, he must see at least one black hat ahead of him.

After it becomes apparent to the middle man that the back man can't figure out what he's wearing, he knows that there is at least one black hat worn by himself and the front man. Knowing this, if the middle man saw a white hat in front of him, he'd know that his own hat was black, and could answer the question correctly. But, since he doesn't answer, he must see a black hat on the front man.

After it becomes apparent to the front man that neither of the men behind him can answer the question, he realizes the middle man saw a black hat in front of him. So he says, correctly, "My hat is black."

19. The boy, the older twin, was born early on March 1st. Then the boat crossed the International Date Line, and the girl was born on February 28th. In a leap year, the younger twin celebrates her birthday two days before her older brother.

20. Start with the assumption that everybody knows their own spouses -- which means that everybody there knew at least one person. Discounting yourself, everyone knows a different number of people, which means that (again, discounting yourself) one person knows one, one person knows two, one person knows three, etc., up to one person who knows nine people (everybody else). Number the people (besides yourself) according to how many people they know, so that person 1 is the one who knows one person, person 2 is the one who knows two people, etc.

Now pair up people with their spouses. If person 9 knows everybody else, s/he must be the only person who knows person 1, because person 1 only knows one person. So they must be married. Person 8 knows everybody except for person 1. Person 2 therefore knows person 8 and person 9. Person 9 is married to person 1, so person 2's spouse must be person 8. Person 7 knows everybody except for persons 1 and 2. Person 3 therefore knows persons 7, 8, and 9. Persons 8 and 9 are married to persons 2 and 1 respectively, so person 3's spouse must be person 7. Person 6 knows everybody except for persons 1, 2, and 3. Person 4 therefore knows persons 6, 7, 8, and 9. The only one of those not yet paired up is person 6, so person 4 and person 6 must be married.

This leaves person 5, who knows everyone except persons 1, 2, 3, and 4. These five people, therefore, must be persons 6, 7, 8, 9, and you. Since you are the only one of these five not yet paired up, person 5 must be your spouse. So your spouse knew five people prior to the party.

The above also determines that the people who know you are persons 5, 6, 7, 8, and 9. So you knew five people prior to the party also.

21. His son.

22. Fill the 8 liter jug with the 12 liter jug, leaving 4 liters remaining. Fill the 5 liter jug with the 8 liter jug, leaving 3 liters remaining. Empty the 5 liter jug into the 12 liter jug. Now there are 9 liters in the 12 liter jug and 3 liters in the 8 liter jug. Pour the 3 liters from the 8 liter jug into the 5 liter jug. Now fill the 8 liter jug with water from the 12 liter jug, leaving 1 liter in the 12 liter jug. Fill the 5 liter jug

(which already has 3 liters in it) from the 8 liter jug, leaving 6 liters in the 8 liter jug. Empty the 5 liter jug into the 12 liter jug. Now there are 6 liters in the 12 liter jug, 6 liters in the 8 liter jug, and the 5 liter jug is empty.

23. Whispered Promises came in first. Skipper's Gal and Happy Go Lucky tied for second place. Penuche Fudge came in fourth. Near Miss came in fifth.

24. This is a tongue twister of an explanation, but bear with me.
The shortest of the tallest people in each row will be taller than, or the same height as, the tallest of the shortest people in each column. There are four cases. The first is that the shortest of the tallest and the tallest of the shortest are the same person, so obviously in this case the shortest of the tallest and the tallest of the shortest would be the same height. The second case is that the shortest of the tallest and the tallest of the shortest are in the same row. The shortest of the tallest people in each row is obviously the tallest person in his row, so he's taller than the tallest of the shortest, who is also in his row. The third case is that the shortest of the tallest and the tallest of the shortest are in the same column. The tallest of the shortest people in each column is obviously the shortest person in his row, so he's shorter than the shortest of the tallest, who is also in his column.
The fourth case is that the shortest of the tallest is neither in the same column nor the same row as the

tallest of the shortest. For this case, consider the person X who is standing in the intersection of the row containing the shortest of the tallest and the column containing the tallest of the shortest. X must be taller than the tallest of the shortest, since the tallest of the shortest is the shortest in his column, and X must also be shorter than the shortest of the tallest, since the shortest of the tallest is the tallest in his row. So TofS < X < SofT.

So the shortest of the tallest in each row is always taller than, or the same height as, the tallest of the shortest in each column.

25. There's the same amount of lemonade in the orange juice as orange juice in the lemonade. Each cup ends with the same volume of liquid that it started with, and there's still an equal amount of each juice between the two cups.

26. Alternate Solution #1
Three: one rose, one tulip, and one daisy.
Alternate Solution #2
Two, neither of which are roses, tulips, or daisies.

27. The big monkey rows a small monkey over; the big monkey comes back. The big monkey rows the other small monkey over; the big monkey comes back. Two humans row over; a human and a small monkey come back. (Now two humans, the big monkey, and a small monkey are on the starting side of the river, and the third human and the second small monkey are on the destination side.) human and the big monkey row over; the human

and a small monkey come back. Two humans row over; the big monkey rows back. (Now all the monkeys are on the starting side of the river, and all the humans are on the destination side.) The big monkey rows a small monkey over; the big monkey comes back. Then the big monkey rows the other small monkey over.

28. Alternate Solution #1
Number the connectors clockwise, with consecutive numbers: 1, 2, 3, 4, 5, 6, 7. Number the holes clockwise, with every other number, then wrapping back around: 1, 3, 5, 7, 2, 4, 6.
Alternate Solution #2
Number the connectors clockwise, with consecutive numbers: 1, 2, 3, 4, 5, 6, 7. Number the holes clockwise, skipping every other hole. The end result will be: 1, 5, 2, 6, 3, 7, 4.

29. Let the five men be represented by A, B, C, D, and E. Let the five dogs be represented by a, b, c, d, and e. Let the dog that can operate the boat be dog a. a, b, and c cross the river. a comes back alone and takes back d. a goes back and says behind while B, C, and D cross the river. Now A, a, E, and e are on the starting shore, and B, b, C, c, D, and d are on the destination shore. D and d return; A and a cross. C and c go back, and C, D, and E cross. Now dogs c, d, and e are on the starting shore, and everyone else is on the destination shore. a goes back and returns with c and d, then goes back and returns with e.

30. Pick one of the men and ask, "If I were to ask you whether the left fork leads to where I'm going, and you chose to answer that question with the same degree of truth as you answer this question, would you then answer 'yes'?"
The truth teller will say "yes" if the left fork leads to where you're going and "no" otherwise. The liar will answer the same, since he will lie about where the left fork leads, and he will lie about lying. The third man may either lie or tell the truth about this one question, but either way he is behaving like either the truthteller or the liar and thus must correctly report the road to your destination.

31. Three birds were seen by one person each, three were seen by each unique pair (Abel-Mabel, Abel-Caleb, and Mabel-Caleb), and one was seen by all three. So seven birds were seen in all, and each person saw a total of four. Hence, all of the birds Caleb saw were yellow. These four birds are: (1) the one Caleb saw alone, (2) the one Caleb saw with Abel, (3) the one Caleb saw with Mabel, and (4) the one all three saw together. This accounts for both of the yellow birds Abel saw, and two of the three yellow birds Mabel saw. The third yellow bird Mabel saw could not have been the one Abel and Mabel saw together, because Abel only saw two yellow birds; so the third yellow bird Mabel saw must have been the one she saw alone.
So five yellow birds were seen (the one Mabel saw, the one Caleb saw, the one Abel and Caleb saw, the one Mabel and Caleb saw, and the one all three

saw), and two non-yellow birds were seen (the one
Abel saw and the one Abel and Mabel saw) by the

32. Adam had his own coat, Bill's hat, Chuck's
gloves, and Dan's cane. Bill had his own coat, Dan's
hat, Adam's gloves, and Chuck's cane. Chuck had
Dan's coat, his own hat, Bill's gloves, and Adam's
cane. Dan had Chuck's coat, Adam's hat, his own
gloves, and Bill's cane.

33. The father is 40, and the son is 10.
34. The two intellectuals in front must be wearing
hats of the same color. Let's suppose the front two
were wearing red hats, the third was wearing a
white hat, and the fourth (in back) was wearing a
blue hat. The intellectual in back must be the first to
answer. If he saw one hat of each color on the three
intellectuals in front of him, he would not be able to
guess the color of his own hat, since the duplicate
color could be any of them. Therefore, he must see
two hats of the same color (red) and one hat of a
second color (white), and he can state conclusively
that he must be wearing the hat of the third color
(blue).
Since the back person can say what color hat he's
wearing, the other intellectuals must realize that no
one else is wearing a hat of that color. So each of
the others can narrow down the color of their own
hats to the remaining two colors.
The next intellectual knows his hat isn't blue, and he
knows there is only one hat that's blue. If he saw a
hat of each of the two remaining colors on the two
intellectuals in front of him, he wouldn't be able to

determine the color of his own hat, since the duplicate color could be either of them. He must, therefore, see two hats of the same color (red), and can conclude that his own hat is of the color he does not see (white).

The next intellectual realizes that the only way the two intellectuals behind him could guess the colors of their hats would be if he and the front intellectual were wearing hats of the same color. He sees the color of the front intellectual's hat (red) and states that this is the color of his.

The front intellectual realizes this too and repeats the color stated by the intellectual behind him.

35. 1 sees 2 and 3. If 1 saw two black hats or two white hats, then he would be able to guess the color of his hat. But in this case, he doesn't -- he sees a white hat and a black hat. Some time passes, and 2 realizes that 1 is not sure what color hat he's wearing. The only way 1 wouldn't be sure is if 2 and 3 are wearing differently colored hats. 2, who sees what color hat 3 is wearing (black), correctly names the opposite color as the color of his own hat.

36. Build three pens and put three pigs in each. Then build a fourth pen around the other three.

37. "You will boil me in oil."

38. The three people are a grandfather, father, and son.

39. Mr. Fast and Mr. Speed cross first, taking two minutes. Mr. Fast returns with the flashlight, taking two minutes. Mr. Slow and Mr. Medium cross, taking ten minutes. Mr. Speed returns with the flashlight, taking one minute. Mr. Fast and Mr. Speed cross again, taking two minutes.

40 The problem can be solved in three weighings. Weigh four marbles against four others, leaving four on the table.

If both sides are equal, all eight marbles on the scale can be eliminated. Put three of the four from the table onto one side and three from the eliminated batch on the other.

If both sides are equal, the odd marble is the last one; weigh it with any other marble to see if it's heavier or lighter.

If the side with the marbles still under consideration moves up or down, weigh one of those three marbles against one of the others, and the third marble is set aside.

If both sides are equal, the third marble is the odd one, and it is heavier or lighter depending on whether or not the scales moved down or up in the previous weighing.

If the scales move, the odd marble is the one that moves in the same direction that the three marbles under consideration moved in the previous weighing. If it moves up, it's lighter; if it moves down, it's heavier.

If the scales move, take one marble from each side and switch them. One one side only, remove the other three and set them aside for later. Replace them with three marbles from the four left on the table (now known not to be the odd one).

If the two sides are equal, the odd marble is among the three set aside. Weigh one against another, and set the third aside.

If the sides are equal, the odd marble is the third one, and it is heavier or lighter depending on which way the scales moved in the first weighing.

If the scales move, the odd marble is the one that moved in the same direction as it did in the first weighing, and it is heavier or lighter depending on whether it went down or up.

If the two sides move in different directions as in the first weighing, the odd marble is one of the two that switched places. Weigh one of the two against any of the other ten.

If both sides are equal, the odd marble is the one left out. It's heavier or lighter depending on which way the scales moved in the second weighing.

If the scales move, the marble on the scales that's under consideration is the odd one, and it is heavier or lighter depending on whether it went down or up.

If the two sides move in the same direction as in the first weighing, the odd marble is one of the three that hadn't moved from its side. Weigh one of the three against another, and set the third aside.

If the sides are equal, the odd marble is the third one, and it is heavier or lighter depending on which way the scales moved in the previous weighings.

If the scales move, the odd marble is the one that moved in the same direction as it did in the previous weighings, and it is heavier or lighter depending on whether it went down or up.

41. Light one fuse at both ends and, at the same time, light the second fuse at one end. When the first fuse has completely burned, you know that a half hour has elapsed, and, more relevantly, that the second fuse has a half hour left to go. At this time,

light the second fuse from the other end. This will cause it to burn out in 15 more minutes. At that point, exactly 45 minutes will have elapsed.

42. Alternate Solution #1

Fill the three-gallon tank from the eight-gallon. Dump the three-gallon tank into the five-gallon. Fill the three-gallon tank from the eight-gallon again and use that to fill the five-gallon. Now you've got two gallons in the eight-gallon tank, five gallons in the five-gallon tank, and one gallon in the three-gallon tank.

Dump the five-gallon tank into the eight-gallon tank. Put the gallon from the three-gallon tank into the five-gallon tank. Now you've got seven gallons in the eight-gallon tank and one in the five-gallon tank. Fill the three-gallon tank from the eight-gallon tank. Dump the three-gallon tank into the five-gallon tank. You should now have four gallons in the eight-gallon tank and four gallons in the five-gallon tank.

Alternate Solution #2

Fill the five-gallon tank from the eight-gallon. Fill the three-gallon tank from the five-gallon. Pour the three-gallon tank back into the eight-gallon tank. Now you should have six gallons in the eight-gallon tank and two gallons in the five-gallon tank.

Dump the two gallons in the five-gallon tank into the three-gallon tank. Pour what you can from the eight-gallon tank into the five-gallon tank. Now you should have one gallon in the eight-gallon tank, five gallons in the five-gallon tank, and two gallons in the three-gallon tank.

Top off the three-gallon tank from the five-gallon, and dump the three-gallon tank into the eight-gallon tank.

43. A won the gold medal; D won the silver medal; C won the bronze medal.

44. Suzy's birthday must be on December 31 of some year. Let's say she was born on December 31, 2000. That means Suzy's ninth birthday is December 31, 2009. And let's say "today" is January 1, 2010.

If we suppose these things, then two days earlier would be December 30, 2009, the day before Suzy's ninth birthday. She was 8.

Now let's get back to today's date, January 1, 2010. "Next year" is 2011. On January 1, 2011, she'll only be 10, but on December 31 that same year, she'll be 11.

45. Yes. No matter how he varies his travel speed within the two trips, there must indeed be such a point somewhere along the path. An easy way to visualize this is to imagine, instead of one man making one trip and then making the return trip, two men making the trip at the same time. One man leaves the bottom at 1pm and heads toward the top. The other leaves the top at 1pm and heads toward the bottom. Regardless of their rate of travel over the course of the trip, they *must* pass each other on their respective journeys -- or, in other words, that at some point they must be at the same place at the same time.

PRACTICAL REASONING
(solutions at end of practical reasoning section)

1. If you put a coin in an empty bottle and insert a cork into the neck of the bottle, how could you remove the coin without taking the cork out or breaking the bottle?

2. You want to send a valuable object to a friend securely. You have a box which can be fitted with multiple locks, and you have several locks and their corresponding keys. However, your friend does not have any keys to your locks, and if you send a key in an unlocked box, the key could be copied en route. How can you send the object securely?

3. You've been sentenced to death in an obscure foreign country which has a strange law. Before the sentence is carried out, two papers -- one with "LIFE" written on it and one with "DEATH" written on it -- are folded up and placed in a hat. You are permitted to pick out one of the papers (without looking), and if you choose the one with "LIFE" written on it, you are set free. Otherwise, the death sentence is carried out. On this occasion, a mean-spirited acquaintance of yours, bent on your demise, has substituted the paper with "LIFE" written on it with another one with "DEATH" written on it. This person gleefully informs you of what he has done and that you are doomed to die. You are not permitted to speak to anyone about this misdeed, nor will you have a chance to switch the

papers or the hat yourself in time. How will you avoid certain death?

4. You have an old-fashioned refrigerator with a small freezer compartment capable of holding seven ice cube trays stacked vertically. But there are no shelves to separate the trays, and if you stack one tray on top of another before the ice cubes in the bottom tray are fully frozen, the top tray will nestle into it, and you won't get full cubes in the bottom tray. You have an unlimited supply of trays, each of which can make a dozen cubes. What's the fastest way to make full-sized ice cubes?

5. Why is it better to have round manhole covers than square ones?

6. Four switches can be turned on or off. One is the lightswitch for the incandescent overhead light in the next room, which is initially off, but you don't know which. The other three switches do nothing. From the room with the switches in it, you can't see whether the light in the next room is turned on or off. You may flip the switches as often and as many times as you like, but once you enter the next room to check on the light, you must be able to say which switch controls the light without flipping the switches any further. (And you can't open the door without entering, either!) How can you determine which switch controls the light?

7. Three surgeons and a clumsy cook go camping in the remote wilderness. The clumsy cook stumbles

over the campfire as he is serving the surgeons, injuring himself and dumping hot stew on the hands of the surgeons. The cook's injuries need surgical treatment. The surgeons' injuries are minor but open. It turns out they brought the equipment necessary for the cook's surgery with them, and they can use the campfire to sterilize the tools. But there are only two rubber gloves. Because of the different surgeons' skills, all three of the surgeons are needed to operate on the cook, in sequence. How can this be done without any of them being exposed to the blood of any of the others?

8. Two fifty foot ropes are suspended from a forty foot ceiling twenty feet apart. You have only a knife. How much of the rope can you steal?

9. Two people are talking on the phone long distance. One is in an East Coast state of the U.S., the other is in a West Coast state of the U.S. The first asks the other, "What time is it?" He hears the answer and says, "That's funny. It's the same time here!" Neither one of them were mistaken about the time. How is this possible?

Solutions for Practical Reasoning Riddles

1. Push the cork into the bottle and shake the coin out.

2. Put the valuable object into the box, secure it with one of your locks, and send the box to your friend. Your friend should then attach one of his own locks and return it. When you receive it again, remove your lock and send it back. Now your friend can unlock his own lock and retrieve the object.

3. After you draw one of the papers, swallow it. The jailer will be forced to check the remaining paper to determine what the one you drew said. The jailer will of course see a paper with "DEATH" written on it, assume you drew the one with "LIFE" written on it, and set you free.

4. You can make 120 cubes (10 full trays) in the time it takes to freeze two trays. First, fill four of the trays with water and turn the other three upside down and use them to space the four apart. That gives you 48 cubes. Next, empty the four trays and put two ice cubes in diagonally opposed corners of each of six of the trays. Fill the remaining holes -- and the entire seventh tray -- with water. Using the ice cubes to hold the trays apart, stack all seven (the seventh tray should go on top), and freeze them. You'll get an additional 72 cubes. You can get 72 cubes for every batch except the first, for which spacer ice cubes are not yet available.

5. A square manhole cover can fall into the hole on the diagonal; a round manhole cover cannot be dropped into the hole.

6. Turn on switches 3 and 4 and wait fifteen minutes or so. Then turn switch 3 off, turn switch 2 on, and enter the room. If the bulb is dark and cool, switch 1 controls it. If the bulb is bright and cool, switch 2 controls it. If the bulb is dark and warm, switch 3 controls it. If the bulb is bright and warm, switch 4 controls it.

7. The first surgeon operates with the first glove (glove A) inside the second glove (glove B). The second surgeon operates using just glove B. The third surgeon operates using glove A, turned inside out, inside glove B.

8. Alternate Solution #1
Almost all of it. First tie the ropes together at the ends. then climb one of the ropes. Tie a loop in the rope as close to the ceiling as possible. Hang from the loop, then cut the rope just below it (but don't drop it, or you'll be stuck on the ceiling). Run the rope through the loop and tie it to your waist. Swing over to the other rope and pull the rope that's going through the loop tight. Cut the other rope as close as possible to the ceiling, holding tight to the end of it. Once the rope is loose, you will swing down below the loop. Let yourself down to the ground by letting the rope out. At the bottom, untie yourself and pull the rope completely through the loop. At this point

you'll have all of the rope except what was used to tie the loop.

Alternate Solution #2

All the rope, provided that the knife is such that: it can support your weight when half the blade is stuck in ceiling, and it can bend at the blade-handle junction without breaking. Climb to top of the first rope, bringing other rope along. At the top, stretch the second rope toward you and circle it around your waist. Cut the first rope at the ceilling, hang on, and swing down on the second rope. Climb back up to the ceiling. Pull up the other end of the second rope, and tie it to the end of the first rope. Loop the tied ropes around the handle of the knife. In one (quick) motion, cut the second rope at the ceiling while pushing the knife into the ceiling. Bend the handle of the knife enough so that the rope won't slip out. Go down, hanging on the double rope with both hands. At the floor, jerk hard to release the knife and the rest of the rope.

Alternate Solution #3

Climb up the first rope, carrying up the end of the second with you. Cut the first rope, flush with the ceiling, swinging down on the second. Climb up the second and cut that flush with the ceiling too, but only part way, until it can just barely hold the rest of your weight. Slowly climb down until you're just short of the bottom. Tie a small loop here and climb up about two feet. Secure the loop about your feet and fall to the ground (roughly three feet). Just before your feet hit the ground the force of the fall will snap the rope at the top.

9. One is in Eastern Oregon (Mountain time); the other in Western Florida (Central time), and the phone call takes place on daylight-savings-time changeover day at 1:30am.

SIMPLE LATERAL THINKING PUZZLES. WHAT IS ACTUALLY TAKING PLACE IN THE SCENE?

1. Adults are holding children, waiting their turn. The children are handed (one at a time, usually) to a man, who holds them while a woman shoots them. If the child is crying, the man tries to stop the crying before the child is shot.

2. A cabin, locked from the inside, is perched on the side of a mountain. It is forced open, and thirty people are found dead inside. They had plenty of food and water.

3. A man marries twenty women in his village but isn't charged with polygamy.

4. A man is alone on an island with no food and no water, yet he does not fear for his life.

5. A woman came home with a bag of groceries, got the mail, and walked into the house. On the way to the kitchen, she went through the living room and looked at her husband, who had blown his brains out. She continued to the kitchen, put away the groceries, and made dinner.

6. Joe wants to go home but can't, because the man in the mask is waiting for him.

7. A dead man lies near a pile of bricks and a beetle on top of a book.

8. At the bottom of the sea there lies a ship worth millions of dollars that may never be recovered.

9. A man is found dead in the arctic with a pack on his back.

10. There is a dead man lying in the desert next to a rock.

11. Bruce wins the race, but he gets no trophy.

12. As a man jumps out of a window, he hears the telephone ring and regrets having jumped.

13. A man walks into a room, shoots, and kills himself.

14. Two people in a room alone. One looks around and realizes he's going to die.

15. A man lies dead in a room with fifty-three bicycles in front of him.

16. Charlie died when the music stopped.

17. A horse jumps over a tower and lands on a man, who disappears.

18. A train pulls into a station, but none of the waiting passengers move.

19. A man pushes a car up to a hotel and tells the owner he's bankrupt.

20. Glass breaks, and George and Gracie are dead.

21. A man rides into town on Friday. He stays three nights and leaves on Friday.

22. Beulah died in the Appalachians, while Craig died at sea. Everyone was much happier with Craig's death.

23. A man was brought before a tribal chief, who asked him a question. If he had known the answer, he probably would have died. He didn't, and lived.

24. Two men are found dead outside of an igloo.

25. A writer with an audience of millions insisted that he was never to be interrupted while writing. After the day when he actually was interrupted, he never wrote again.

26. Mr. Black asks for tea and gets $5,000. Then he asks for eyes, but Mrs. White can't give him any.

27. A young woman is whisked away to a far off land, where she kills the first person she meets. Then she teams up with three others to kill again.

SOLUTIONS FOR: SIMPLE LATERAL THINKING PUZZLES

1. Alternate Solution #1
Kids are getting their pictures taken with Santa.
Alternate Solution #2
The man is a doctor, and the woman is a nurse who is giving the children injections.

2. It was an airplane cabin; the plane crashed into the mountain.

3. He's a priest -- he's marrying them to other people, not to himself.

4. The island is a traffic island.

5. The husband had killed himself some time ago; the wife was looking at his ashes in an urn on the mantelpiece.

6. A baseball game is going on. The base-runner sees the catcher waiting at home plate with the ball, so decides to stay at third base to avoid being tagged out.

7. The man was an amateur mechanic, the book is a Volkswagen service manual, the beetle is a car, and the pile of bricks is what the car fell off.

8. The Eagle landed in the Sea of Tranquility and will likely remain there for the foreseeable future.

9. It's a wolf pack; they killed him.

10. The dead man is Superman; the rock is Green Kryptonite.

11. Bruce is a horse.

12. This is a post-holocaust scenario of some kind; for whatever reason, the man believes himself to be the last human on Earth. He doesn't want to live by himself, so he jumps -- but when he hears the telephone ring, he realizes he's not the last human on Earth after all.

13. The man walks into a casino and goes to the craps table. He bets all the money he owns, shoots craps, and loses. Now flat broke, he becomes despondent and commits suicide.

14. It's nighttime. The one who looks around sees his own reflection in the window, but not his companion's. He realizes the other is a vampire.

15. The "bicycles" are Bicycle playing cards; the man was cheating at cards, and when the extra card was found, he was killed by the other players.

16. Charlie was an insect sitting on a chair. The music was being played for a game of musical chairs.

17. Alternate Solution #1
It's a chess game -- knight takes pawn.
Alternate Solution #2

More of an alternate question than an alternate solution -- the problem could be stated this way instead: "Two monks sit in a tower. The queen kills the king. The monks shake hands and part company." The answer, of course, is that the monks were playing chess, and one beat the other.

18. It's a model train set.

19. It's a game of Monopoly.

20. George and Gracie are goldfish; their tank broke.

21. Friday is a horse.

22. Beulah and Craig were hurricanes.

23. The native chief asked him, "What is the third baseman's name in the Abbott and Costello routine 'Who's on First'?" The man, who had no idea, said "I don't know," the correct answer. However, he was a big smart aleck, so if he had known the answer he would have pointed out that "What" was the *second* baseman's name. The chief, being quite humorless, would have executed him on the spot.

24. The men have gone spelunking and have taken an Igloo cooler with them so they can have a picnic down in the caves. They cleverly used dry ice to keep their beer cold, not realizing that as the dry ice sublimed (went from a solid state to a vapor state) it would push the lighter oxygen out of the cave, and they would suffocate.

25. He was a skywriter whose plane crashed into another plane.

26. Mr. Black is a contestant on the game show *Wheel of Fortune*.

27. The young woman is Dorothy, and the story is *The Wizard of Oz*.

ASSOCIATED WORDS

1.
back
short
watch

2.
blue
cake
cottage

3.
stool
 powder
ball

4. .
big
soil
table

5.
made
cuff
left

6.
motion
poke
down

7.
light

hot
check

8.
light
hot
back

9.
wood
liquor
luck

10.
drop
off
stand

11.
car
top
ice

12.
out
baby
out

13.
key
wall
precious

14.
corn
winner
sweet

15
top
inner
test

16.
go
there
seen

17
back
crawl
work

18.
read
child
water

19.
blue
lands
roots

20.
butter
maid

run

21.
hot
strong
arrow

22.
sore
witness
buck

23.
battle
work
play

24.
off
crow
tactics

25.
reading
stick
fat

26.
hook
jelly
bowl

27.

hay
smoke
up

28.
dog
frog
fighter

29.
weight
fly
sand

30.
above
floor
walk

31.
watch
house
gone

32.
hard
under
up

33.
fitting
land
free

34.
salt
melon
white

35.
gum
kick
tear

36.
house
star
street

37.
cart
fifth
chair

38.
theme
trailer
ball

39.
thumb
ever
onion

40.
hog

board
mouth

41.
video
board
waiting
 42.
cheese
guitar
along

43
master
wedding
side

44.
oil
rattle
eyes

45.
rocket
night
lark

46.
neck
snapping
dove

SOLUTIONS FOR ASSOCIATED WORDS

1.
backstop
shortstop
stopwatch
2.
blue cheese
cheesecake
cottage cheese
3.
footstool
foot powder
football
4.
big top
topsoil
tabletop
5.
handmade
handcuff
left-hand
6.
slow motion
slowpoke
slowdown
7.
spotlight
hot spot
spot check
8.
flashlight
hot flash

flashback
9.
hardwood
hard liquor
hard luck
10.
drop kick
kickoff
kickstand
11.
boxcar
boxtop
icebox
12.
outcry
crybaby
cry out
13.
keystone
stone wall
precious stone
14.
cornbread
breadwinner
sweetbread
15.
tube top
innertube
test-tube
16.
forego
therefore
foreseen

17.
backspace
crawlspace
workspace
18.
proofread
childproof
waterproof
19.
bluegrass
grasslands
grass roots
20.
buttermilk
milkmaid
milk run
21.
hothead
headstrong
arrowhead
22.
eyesore
eye witness
buckeye
23.
battleground
groundwork
playground
24.
scare off
scarecrow
scare tactics
25.

lipreading
lipstick
fat lip
26.
fishhook
jellyfish
fishbowl
27.
haystack
smokestack
stack up
28.
bulldog
bullfrog
bullfighter
29.
paperweight
flypaper
sandpaper
30.
above board
floorboard
boardwalk
31.
watchdog
doghouse
doggone
32.
hardcover
undercover
cover up
33.
form-fitting

land form
free form
34.
salt water
watermelon
white water
35.
gumdrop
drop kick
teardrop
36.
lighthouse
starlight
streetlight
37.
cartwheel
fifth wheel
wheelchair
38.
theme park
trailer park
ball park
39.
green thumb
evergreen
green onion
40.
hogwash
washboard
mouthwash
41.
video game
gameboard

waiting game
42.
string cheese
guitar string
string along
43.
ringmaster
wedding ring
ringside
44.
snake oil
rattlesnake
snake eyes
45.
skyrocket
night sky
skylark
46.
turtleneck
snapping turtle
turtledove

LATERAL THINKING DEATH STORYS. GET MORBIDLY CREATIVE WITH YOUR FRIENDS!

1. A man lives on the twelfth floor of an apartment building. Every morning he takes the elevator down to the lobby and leaves the building. In the evening, he gets into the elevator, and, if there is someone else in the elevator -- or if it was raining that day -- he goes back to his floor directly. Otherwise, he goes to the tenth floor and walks up two flights of stairs to his apartment.

2. In the middle of the ocean is a yacht. Several corpses are floating in the water nearby.

3. A man is lying dead in a room. There is a large pile of gold and jewels on the floor, a chandelier attached to the ceiling, and a large open window.

4. A man and his wife raced through the streets. They stopped, and the husband got out of the car. When he came back, his wife was dead, and there was a stranger in the car.

5. A body is discovered in a park in Chicago in the middle of summer. It has a fractured skull and many other broken bones, but the cause of death was hypothermia.

6. A woman has incontrovertible proof in court that her husband was murdered by her sister. The judge declares, "This is the strangest case I've ever seen. Though it's a cut-and-dried case, this woman cannot be punished."

7. A man walks into a bar and asks for a drink. The bartender pulls out a gun and points it at him. The man says, "Thank you," and walks out.

8. A hunter aimed his gun carefully and fired. Seconds later, he realized his mistake. Minutes later, he was dead.

9. A man is returning from Switzerland by train. If he had been in a non-smoking car he would have died.

10. A man goes into a restaurant, orders albatross, eats one bite, and kills himself.

11. A man is found hanging in an otherwise empty locked room with a puddle of water under his feet.

12. A man is dead in a puddle of blood and water on the floor of an otherwise empty locked room.

13. A man is lying dead, face down in the desert. He's wearing a backpack

14. A man is lying dead, face down in the desert. There's a match near his outstretched hand.

15. A man is driving his car. He turns on the radio, listens for five minutes, turns around, goes home, and shoots his wife.

16. A man is driving his car. He turns on the radio, then pulls over to the side of the road and shoots himself.

17. The music stops, and a woman dies.

18. A man is dead in a room with a small pile of wood chips and sawdust in the corner.

19. There's a flash of light, and a man dies.

20. A rope breaks. A bell rings. A man dies.

21. A man is lying drowned in a dead forest.

22. A woman buys a new pair of shoes, goes to work, and dies.

23. A man meets a one armed man on a subway, who pulls a gun and shoots him.

24. A man is lying awake in bed. He makes a phone call, says nothing, and goes to sleep.

25. A man kills his wife, then goes inside his house and kills himself.

26. Two men enter a bar. They are served identical drinks. One lives; the other dies.

27. Joe, wearing a mask and carrying an empty sack, leaves his house. An hour later he returns with a full sack. He goes into a room and turns out the lights.

28. Hans and Fritz are German spies during World War II. They try to enter America, posing as returning tourists. Hans is immediately arrested.

29. Tim and Greg were talking. Tim said, "The terror of flight." Greg said, "The gloom of the grave." Greg was arrested.

30. A man dies of thirst in his own home.

31. A man gets onto an elevator. When the elevator stops, he knows his wife is dead.

32. A man is running along a corridor with a piece of paper in his hand. The lights flicker, and the man drops to his knees and cries out, "Oh no!"

33. A car without a driver moves; a man dies.

34. A woman throws something out a window and dies.

35. An avid birdwatcher sees an unexpected bird. Soon, they're both dead.

36. There are a carrot, a pile of pebbles, and a pipe lying together in the middle of a field.

37. An ordinary American citizen, with no passport, visits over thirty foreign countries in one day. He is welcomed in each country and leaves each one of his own accord.

38. A man is found dead in an alley lying in a red pool with a stick near his head.

39. A man lies dead next to a feather.

40. A man wakes up one night to get some water. He turns off the light and goes back to bed. The next morning he looks out the window, screams, and kills himself.

41. She grabbed his ring, pulled on it, and dropped it, thereby saving his life.

42. A man sitting on a park bench reads a newspaper article headlined "Death at Sea" and knows a murder has been committed.

43. A man drives down the highway at 55 miles per hour. He passes three cars going 60 miles per hour, then gets pulled over by a police officer and is given a ticket.

44. A man tries the new cologne his wife gave him for his birthday. He goes out to get some food and is killed.

45. A man is doing his job when his suit tears. Ten seconds later, he's dead.

46. A man is doing his job when his suit tears. Three minutes later, he's dead.

47. A married couple goes to a movie. During the movie the husband strangles the wife. He is able to get her body home without attracting attention.

48. Mr. Browning is glad the car ran out of gas.

49. A man is sitting suspended over two pressurized containers. Suddenly, he dies.

50. A man leaves a motel room, goes to his car, honks the horn, and returns.

51. Two dead people sit in their cars on a street.

52. A man ran into a fire and lived. A man stayed where there was no fire and died.

53. Three men die. On the pavement are pieces of ice and broken glass.

54. A man ate some food that was not poisoned, yet nevertheless caused him to die.

55. One of Johnny's dearest loved ones binds him to a chair, but Johnny doesn't mind.

56. Two people in a room alone. One looks around and realizes he's going to die.

57. A woman tells her children to do something, but just one boy obeys. The woman says something to him, and he stomps away, sits down, and sulks.

58. A woman tries to drop a man into the ocean -- by his own request -- but when she tries, he blows back in.

SOULTIONS TO: LATERAL THINKING DEATH STORYS

1. The man is a dwarf. He can't reach the upper elevator buttons, but he can ask people to push them for him. He can also push them with his umbrella.

2. Alternate Solution #1

A group of people were on an ocean voyage in a yacht. One day, they decided to go swimming -- they put on their swimsuits and dove off the side. They discovered belatedly that they have forgotten to put a ladder down the side of the yacht and were unable to climb back in, so they drowned.

Alternate Solution #2

The same situation, but they set out a ladder that was just barely long enough. When they dove into the water, the boat, without their weight, rose slightly in the water, putting the ladder just out of reach.

3. The room is the ballroom of an ocean liner which sank some time ago. The man ran out of air while diving in the wreck.

4. The wife was about to have a baby. They drove to the hospital. The husband left to get a wheelchair, but the baby was born in the meantime, and the wife didn't survive the birth.

5. A poor peasant from somewhere in Europe desperately wants to come to the United States. Lacking money for airfare, he stows away in the landing gear compartment of a jet. He dies of hypothermia in mid-flight and falls out when the compartment opens as the plane makes its final approach.

6. The sisters are Siamese twins

7. The man has hiccups; the bartender scares them away by pulling a gun.

8. Alternate Solution #1

It was winter. He fired the gun near a snowy cliff, which started an avalanche.

Alternate Solution #2

He shot an elephant with a low caliber rifle. Not powerful enough to kill it, the elephant became enraged and trampled him.

9. The man used to be blind -- he's returning from an eye operation which restored his sight. He spent all his money on the operation, so when the train (which had no internal lighting) goes through a tunnel, he thinks he's gone blind again and decides to kill himself. But before he could do it, he saw the light of the cigarettes people were smoking and realized he could still see.

10. The man, his wife, and a second man were in a ship that was wrecked on a desert island. The man's wife died in the wreck. When there was no food left, the second man brought what he said was an albatross but was really part of the dead wife. Later they were rescued, and at some point, the first man decides to order albatross at a restaurant. It tastes nothing like what he was told was albatross on the island, which makes him realize he really ate his wife. Unable to cope with the realization, he kills himself.

11. He stood on a block of ice to hang himself.

12. He stabbed himself with an icicle.

13. He jumped out of an airplane, but his parachute failed to open.

14. He was with several others in a hot air balloon, crossing the desert. The balloon was punctured, and they began to lose altitude. They tossed all their non-essentials overboard and then their clothing and food, but they were still sinking too fast. They drew matches to see who would jump over the side and save the others. This man lost.

15. The radio program is one of those shows where they call up someone at random and ask them a question. The announcer states the name and town of the man's wife as the person he would call next. He does so, and a male voice answers. From this, he gathered his wife was having an affair.

16. He's a DJ at a radio station and decides he wants to kill his wife. To establish his alibi, he puts a prerecorded record on the air, quickly drives home, and kills her. On the way back, he turns on his show and discovers the record is skipping.

17. The woman is a tightrope walker in a circus. Her act consists of walking the rope blindfolded, accompanied by music, without a net. The conductor is supposed to stop the music when she reaches the end of the rope, signaling that it's safe to step off onto the platform. That day, the usual conductor was ill. The substitute stopped the music early.

18. The man is a blind dwarf, the shortest one in the circus. Another dwarf, jealous because he's not as short, has been sawing small pieces off the other's cane every night. When he uses his cane each morning, it appears to him that he's grown taller. Since his only income is from being a circus midget, he decides to kill himself when he gets too tall.

19. Alternate Solution #1

The man is struck by lightning.

Alternate Solution #2

The man is a lion-tamer, posing for a photo with his lions. The lions react badly to the flash of the camera, and the man is momentarily blinded by it, so he gets mauled.

20. Alternate Solution #1

A blind man enjoys walking near a cliff and uses the sound of a buoy to gauge his distance from the edge. One day the buoy's anchor rope breaks, allowing the buoy to drift away from the shore. When it rings, the man thinks he's further away from the edge than he is, walks over it, and falls to his death.

Alternate Solution #2

The man is a bell ringer. One day the rope breaks, and he falls down the shaft and dies.

21. He was scuba diving when a firefighting plane landed nearby and filled its tanks with water, sucking him in. He ran out of air while the plane was in flight; then the water, with him in it, was dumped onto a burning forest.

22. The woman is the assistant to a circus knife-thrower, who stands in front of a target as knives are thrown around her. The new shoes have higher heels than she normally wears, causing the thrower to misjudge his aim.

23. These two men, along with several others, were shipwrecked on a desert island and had run out of food. The men agreed that they needed to eat their arms to survive, but that it if one person had to lose his arm to save them, they should all lose their arms.

The men were rescued before the last man's arm was eaten; this man ran away before he could be caught and forced to give up his arm. However, he bumped into one of the other survivors in the subway one day, who killed him for not living up to his end of the bargain.

24. He is in a hotel and is unable to sleep because the man in the adjacent room is snoring. He calls the snorer up (at this hotel, like many others, the phone numbers are based on the room number). The snorer wakes up and answers. The first man hangs up without saying anything and goes to sleep before the snorer starts snoring again.

25. It's the man's fiftieth birthday, and in celebration of this he plans to kill his wife and move to a new life in another state. His wife takes him out to dinner; afterward, on their front step, he kills her. He opens the door, dragging her body in with him, and suddenly all the lights turn on and a group of his friends shout, "Surprise!" Caught red-handed, the man kills himself.

26. The drinks contain poisoned ice cubes; one man drinks slowly, giving them time to melt, while the other drinks quickly and thus doesn't get much of the poison.

27. Joe is a kid who goes trick-or-treating for Halloween, returns, and goes to sleep.

28. Crossing the border, Hans and Fritz were required to fill out a personal information form, which asked, among other things, their birthdays. The German date ordering is day/month/year, rather than the American way, month/day/year. Fritz was born on, say, July 7th, so he wrote down 7/7/15 --

no problem. Hans was born on, say, July 20th, so he wrote down 20/7/15 instead of the American way, 7/20/15. Since Hans had claimed to be a returning American, he was found out by the border police.

29. Greg is a German spy during World War II. Tim, an American, is suspicious of him, so he plays a word-association game with him. When Tim says, "The land of the free," Greg says, "The home of the brave." When Tim says, "The terror of flight," Greg says, "The gloom of the grave." Any U.S. citizen would know the first verse of the national anthem, but only a spy would have memorized the third.

30. His home is a houseboat, and he has run out of water while on an extended cruise.

31. He's leaving a hospital after visiting his wife, who's on a life support system. The power goes out, stopping the elevator and, he guesses, the life support system, too. (He assumes if the emergency backup generator were working, the elevator wouldn't lose power either.)

32. The man is delivering a pardon, and the flicker of the lights indicates that the person to be pardoned has just been electrocuted.

33. The murderer sets the car on a slope above the hot dog stand where the victim works. He wedges an ice block in the car to keep the brake pedal down, puts the car in neutral, and flies to another city to avoid suspicion. It's a warm day; when the ice melts, the car rolls down the hill and kills the hot dog man.

34. The object she throws is a boomerang. It flies out, loops around, comes back, and hits her in the head.

35. He is a passenger in an airplane and sees the bird get sucked into an engine at 20,000 feet. The engine stalls, and the plane crashes.

36. They're the remains of a melted snowman

37. He is a mail courier who delivers packages to the different foreign embassies in the United States. The land of an embassy belongs to the country of the embassy, not to the United States.

38. The man died from eating a poisoned popsicle.

39. The man was a sword swallower in a carnival side show. While he was practicing, someone tickled his throat with the feather, causing him to gag.

40. The man is a lighthouse keeper. He wasn't quite awake when he got up in the night -- unwittingly, he had shut off the light in the lighthouse. During the night, a ship crashes on the rocks. When the man realized what he had done, he killed himself.

41. They were skydiving. He broke his arm as he jumped from the plane by hitting it on the plane door, and he couldn't reach his ripcord with his other arm. She pulled the ripcord for him.

42. The man is a travel agent. He had sold someone two tickets for an ocean voyage, one round-trip and one one-way. The last name of the man who bought the tickets is the same as the last name of the woman who "fell" overboard and drowned on the voyage, which is the subject of the article he's reading.

43. The man was driving the wrong way on a one way street.

44. The man is a beekeeper, and the bees attack en masse because they don't recognize his fragrance.

45. The man works at a factory. His clothing got caught on a piece of machinery, dragged him in, and killed him.

46. The man is an astronaut out on a space walk.

47. The movie is at a drive-in theater.

48. Mr. and Mrs. Browning had just gotten married. Mrs. Browing was subject to fits of depression. They had their first fight soon after they were married; Mr. Browning stormed out of the house, and Mrs. Browning went into the garage and started up the car, intending to kill herself by filling the garage with car exhaust. But the car ran out of gas quickly, and Mr. Browning, returning home to apologize, found Mrs. Browning in time to summon help and restore her to health.

49. He's riding a bicycle or motorcycle, and he crashes and dies.

50. It's the middle of the night. The man goes outside to get something from his car, but forgets which room he was in. His wife is deaf, so he honks the car horn loudly, waking up everyone else in the motel. The other residents all get up and turn on their lights, and the man returns to the one room that remains dark.

51. Because there was a heavy fog, two people driving in opposite directions on the same road both stuck their heads out of their windows to see the center line better. Their heads hit each other at high speed, killing them both.

52. The two men were working in a small room protected by a carbon dioxide gas fire extinguisher system, when a fire broke out in an adjoining room. One of the men ran through the fire and escaped

with only minor burns. The other one stayed in the room until the fire extinguishers kicked in and died of oxygen starvation.

53. A large man takes the elevator from the ground floor to the third floor penthouse apartment he shares with his wife. After greeting her, he sees a man's watch on the table and assumes she's been having an affair. Thinking her boyfriend has escaped down the stairs, he rushes to the French windows and sees a good-looking man just leaving the main entrance of the building. Furious, the husband pushes the refrigerator through the window onto the young man below. The young man is killed by the refrigerator. The husband is killed from a heart attack caused by overexertion. The wife's boyfriend, who was hiding inside the refrigerator, is killed from the fall.

54. Alternate Solution #1

A man choked to death on a fried chicken leg.

Alternate Solution #2

The man was Adam, and eating the forbidden fruit was punished by God making him mortal...so that he'd ultimately die.

55. Johnny is a kid. The chair is a seat in a car. One of Johnny's parents put his seatbelt on for him.

56. The two people are Siamese twins. One wakes up, notices that the other one is dead, and realizes he will die soon, too.

57. The woman is playing a game of "Simon Says" with her children.

58. The man has been cremated. The woman is his wife. Before his death, he requested that his ashes

be scattered on the ocean. But it's a windy day, and his ashes blow back on the boat.

JOKE RIDDLES. DO YOU HAVE COMMON SENSE?

1. Suppose you are on an elevator on the 16th floor of a building, when the cable breaks. As you plummet toward the ground, you recall that you once heard that by jumping up *fast* at the instant of impact, you can escape death. You also recall that the floors are twelve feet apart and that the acceleration of a falling object is 32 feet per second squared. When should you jump?

2. A dog can run fifty miles in a day. How far could he run into a 120 square mile forest in two days?

3. A light year is 5.9x10^12 miles and Alpha Centuri is 2.5x10^14 miles away. If your friend stood on the surface of Alpha Centuri and waved, how long would it be until you could see it from the earth?

4. Buildings A and B are adjacent buildings. The floors in the buildings are twelve feet apart. Building B is 16 stories high. If Gumball the Clown jumped out of the 20th story window of Building A, how far would he fall before hitting the roof of Building B?

5. If you roll snake eyes eight times in a row with the same pair of dice, what is the chance of rolling snake eyes on your ninth roll?

6. The human body holds nine quarts of blood. Suppose you were alone in the desert and accidently cut a major artery. If you bleed at one cup a minute, how long will it take you to bleed to death?

7. What's the largest number of coins you can have without having even change for a dollar?

8. If a boy and a half could eat a hot dog and a half in a minute and a half, how many hot dogs could six boys eat in six minutes?

SOLUTIONS TO JOKE RIDDLES

1. You would impact between the 2nd and 3rd second after the cable broke, so you would want to jump 2 seconds after the break. However, considering the calculations involved, you would probably end up as a heap of screaming bloody mess at the bottom of the elevator shaft before you figured the answer out. Besides, there's no telling if jumping really works.

2. About half way. After that, he starts running out of the woods.

3. From now until hell freezes over. No telescope yet invented has *that* kind of magnification. Besides, Alpha Centuri is a star and your friend couldn't get within miles of it without being vaporized.

4. Far enough

5. Pretty damn good! The dice are obviously loaded.

6. Apply a tourniquet, and you won't.

7. As many as you can carry, if they aren't in dollar-based currencies.

8. Who cares? I want to see how that half a boy can eat anything.

MORE COMMON SENSE JOKE RIDDLES

1. I have two U.S. coins that add up to fifty-five cents. One is not a nickel. What coins are they?

2. A farmer had nine sheep, and all but seven died. How many did he have left?

3. Three large people try to crowd under one small umbrella, but nobody gets wet. How is this possible?

4. You are a bus driver. At the first stop of the day, eight people get on board. At the second stop, four get off, and eleven get on. At the third stop, two get off, and six get on. At the fourth stop, thirteen get off, and one gets on. At the fifth stop, five get off, and three get on. At the sixth stop, three get off, and two get on. What color are the bus driver's eyes?

5. If you take two apples from three apples, how many do you have?

6. A certain five letter word becomes shorter when you add two letters to it. What is the word?

7. An electric train is traveling northwest at 95 miles per hour, and the wind is blowing southwest at 95 miles per hour. In which direction does the smoke blow?

8. Some months have 30 days. Some months have 31 days. How many months have 28 days?

9. A train leaves from New York City heading toward Los Angeles at 100 mph. Three hours later, a train leaves from Los Angeles heading toward New York City at 200 mph. Assume there's exactly 2000 miles between Los Angeles and New York City. When they meet, which train is closer to New York City?

10. A woman gave birth to two sons who were born on the same hour of the same day of the same year but were not twins. How is this possible?

11. A man lives in a house with four walls. Each wall has a window. Each window has a southern exposure. A bear walks by. What color is the bear?

12. Your sock drawer contains ten pairs of white socks and ten pairs of black socks. If you're only allowed to take one sock from the drawer at a time, what's the minimum number of socks you need to take before you're guaranteed to have a pair?

13. A black man dressed all in black, wearing a black mask, stands at a crossroads in a totally black-painted town. All of the streetlights in town are broken. There is no moon. A black-painted car without headlights drives straight toward him, but turns in time and doesn't hit him. How did the driver know to swerve?

14. A man was born in 1964 and died in 1984 at the age of 25. How is this possible?

15. A horse is tied to a 30 foot rope. A haystack lies 40 feet away, but the horse is able to eat it. How is this possible?

16. Forward I'm heavy, backwards I'm not. What am I?

17. What two words have the most letters in it?

18. While on my way to St. Ives,
I met a man with seven wives.
Each wife had seven sacks;
Each sack had seven cats;
Each cat had seven kittens.
Kittens, cats, sacks, wives;
How many were going to St. Ives?

19. An encyclopedia consists of ten volumes (sitting next to each other, in order, on a shelf). Each volume contains one thousand pages. Excluding the covers of each volume, how many pages are between the first page of the encyclopedia and the last?

20. If a boy and a half can eat a hot dog and a half in a minute and a half, how long would it take six boys to eat six hot dogs?

21. How long is the answer to this question?

22. What do you call a man who was born in Columbus, raised in Cincinnati, and died in Chicago?

23. How many outs in an inning?

24. How many birthdays does the average man have?

25. If you had one match and entered a room in which there were a kerosene lamp, an oil burner, and a wood burning stove, which would you light first?

26. If a doctor gave you three pills and told you to take one every half hour, how long would they last you?

27. An archeologist claims he found some gold coins dated 46 B.C. Do you believe him?

28. Is it legal for a man living west of the Mississippi River to be buried east of the Mississippi River?

29. Divide 30 by 1/2 and add 10. What is the answer?

30. How many animals of each gender did Moses take aboard the ark?

31. A clerk in a butcher's shop is five foot ten. What does he weigh?

32. Do they have a 4th of July in England?

33. In North Carolina, is it legal for a man to marry his widow's sister?

34. A man leaves home and takes three left turns. Upon arriving back home he comes across two men wearing masks. Who are these men?

35. How can you take 1 from 19 and leave 20?

36. Jack gave John the following challenge: "If you sit down in that chair, I bet I can make you get out of it before I run around the chair three times," he said.

"Aw, that's not fair," John said. "You'll just prick me with a pin or something."

"Nope," Jack said. "I won't touch you, either directly or with any object. If you get out of the chair, it'll be by your own choice."

John thought, accepted the challenge, and lo and behold, Jack won the bet. How did he do it?

37. How much dirt is there in a hole in the ground that's two feet wide, three feet long, and four feet deep?

38. A strong man at the circus can bench press 1200 pounds. How much can he lift with a pulley and a 25 foot rope when the rope weighs two pounds, the pulley is attached to the ceiling, the ceiling is 10 feet from the floor, and the man is standing on the floor?

39. How many grooves are there on an LP record?

40. What word is always spelled incorrectly?

41. On what day(s) of the year does the sun rise and set at the same time of day?

42. Think of words ending in "gry." Angry and hungry are two of them. There are only three words in the English language. What is the third word?

The word is something that everyone uses every day. If you have listened carefully, I have already told you what it is.

43. If eggs can be laid at the rate of eight every seven days, how many can a rooster lay in sixteen days?

44. George's mother had three children: one named April, one named May, and one named what?

45. You are competing in a race and overtake the runner in second place. Which position are in you now?

46. A woman has seven children. Half of them are boys. How is this possible?

47. How many 3-cent stamps in a dozen?

48. A rope ladder is hanging over the side of a ship. The ladder is 12 feet long, and the rungs are one foot apart. The lowest rung is resting on the top of the ocean. The tide rises at the rate of four inches per hour. How long will it take before the first four rungs of the ladder are under water?

49. Which would be worth more - a trunk full of nickels or a half a trunk full of dimes?

50. In a group of siblings, there are seven sisters, and each sister has one brother. How many siblings are there in total?

SOLUTIONS TO: MORE COMMON SENSE JOKE RIDDLES

1. A nickel and a half dollar. Only one is not a nickel.
2. Seven.
3. The sun is shining; there's no rain.
4. Whatever color yours are. You're the bus driver.
5. Two.
6. Short.
7. There isn't any smoke. It's an electric train.
8. All of them.
9. Alternate Solution #1
When they meet, they're both exactly the same distance from New York City.
Alternate Solution #2
Well, actually if you consider "meeting" to be nose to nose, the one that left from New York City is closer to New York City by a train length.
10. They were two of triplets.
11. The only place each window could have a southern exposure is on the north pole. So the bear must have been a polar bear. The answer, therefore, is white.
12. Two. Nobody said it had to be a matching pair.
13. It's daytime; the sun is out.
14. He's born in room number 1964 of a hospital and dies in room number 1984.
15. Alternate Solution #1
The other end of the rope isn't tied to anything.
Alternate Solution #2
The haystack is only 10 feet away from where the other end of the rope is tied, and the horse is 30 feet away on the other side.

16. A ton.

17. Post Office.

18. One. Everybody else was coming *from* St. Ives.

19. Eight thousand. When books sit on shelves, the first page of the book is the rightmost page, and the last page is the leftmost page. So you can't count the pages in the first and last volumes.

20. A minute and a half.

21. Alternate Solution #1

Ten letters.

Alternate Solution #2

Nineteen letters long.

Alternate Solution #3

Twenty five letters in length.

Alternate Solution #4

Two words.

Alternate Solution #5

Three words long.

Alternate Solution #6

Four words in length.

Alternate Solution #7

Four syllables.

Alternate Solution #8

Five syllables long.

Alternate Solution #9

Six syllables in length.

Alternate Solution #10

The answer is one sentence long.

Alternate Solution #11

How long.

22. Dead.

23. Six. (Three for each team.)

24. One.

25. The match.

26. An hour. You take one right away, take the next a half hour later, and the last one a half hour after that.

27. I don't. In 46 B.C., they wouldn't have known how many years before Christ it was.

28. Not if he isn't dead yet.

29. 70. (30 divided by 2 is 15, but 30 divided by 1/2 is 60.)

30. None. Noah was the one with the ark.

31. Meat.

32. Of course. They just don't celebrate it.

33. No. If he has a widow, he's dead.

34. The umpire and the catcher.

35. When the numbers are expressed in roman numerals, this works out:
If you take I from XIX, you are left with XX.

36. John sat down in the chair. Jack ran around it twice, then said, "I'll be back in a week to run the third time around!"

37. None.

38. No more than his own weight.

39. Just two -- one on each side.

40. Incorrectly.

41. The sun never rises and sets at the same time of day. Except at the poles, the sun only rises in the morning and only sets in the evening. Even at the poles, it can't do both simultaneously.

42. "Language." Ignore the first two sentences, which are irrelevant to the question. The third sentence says, "There are three words in 'the English language.'" The first is "the"; the second is

"English"; and the third is "language." Language is something we use every day.

Unfortunately, this puzzle is frequently asked of others by those who do not know the answer; as such, the wording of the puzzle is inadvertently altered in such a way that there is no correct answer. There *are* a couple other archaic words in English that end in "gry"; however, none of these are correct answers, because none of them are things we use every day. (Besides, then the puzzle would be a trivia question rather than a riddle.)

43. None. Roosters do not lay eggs.

44. George.

45. Second.

46. They're *all* boys. Half are boys, and so is the other half.

47. 12

48. They will never be under water. The ship will rise with the tide.

49. Alternate Solution #1

Half a trunk full of dimes. Dimes are worth twice as much, so half the number of dimes as nickels would be worth the same amount. But since dimes are smaller than nickels, more dimes than nickels can fit in the same amount of space.

Alternate Solution #2

Depends on whether the trunk was cut in half horizontally or vertically. Vertically, you couldn't carry many dimes are in it, so the whole trunk full of nickels is probably the better bet.

50. Eight: seven sisters and one brother.

27791482R00053

Made in the USA
Lexington, KY
23 November 2013